CAN I CHANGE THE WAY I LOOK?

A Teen's Guide
to the Health Implications of
Cosmetic Surgery, Makeovers,
and Beyond

The Science of Health: Youth and Well-Being

Taking Responsibility
A Teen's Guide to Contraception and Pregnancy

Staying Safe
A Teen's Guide to Sexually Transmitted Diseases

What Do I Have to Lose?
A Teen's Guide to Weight Management

Balancing Act
A Teen's Guide to Managing Stress

Surviving the Roller Coaster
A Teen's Guide to Coping with Moods

Clearing the Haze
A Teen's Guide to Smoking-Related Health Issues

Right on Schedule!
A Teen's Guide to Growth and Development

The Best You Can Be
A Teen's Guide to Fitness and Nutrition

The Silent Cry
Teen Suicide and Self-Destructive Behaviors

Breathe Easy!
A Teen's Guide to Allergies and Asthma

Can I Change the Way I Look?
A Teen's Guide to the Health Implications of
Cosmetic Surgery, Makeovers, and Beyond

Taking Care of Your Smile
A Teen's Guide to Dental Care

Dead on Their Feet
Teen Sleep Deprivation and Its Consequences

Dying for Acceptance
A Teen's Guide to Drug- and Alcohol-Related Health Issues

For All to See
A Teen's Guide to Healthy Skin

CAN I CHANGE THE WAY I LOOK?

A Teen's Guide
to the Health Implications of
Cosmetic Surgery, Makeovers,
and Beyond

by Autumn Libal

Mason Crest Publishers
Philadelphia

Mason Crest Publishers Inc.
370 Reed Road, Broomall, Pennsylvania 19008
(866) MCP-BOOK (toll free)
www.masoncrest.com

ISBN 1-59084-840-3 (series)

Library of Congress Cataloging-in-Publication Data

Libal, Autumn.
  Can I change the way I look? : a teen's guide to the health implica-tions of cosmetic surgery, makeovers, and beyond / by Autumn Libal.
      p. cm. —(The science of health)
  Includes index.
  ISBN 1-59084-843-8
  1. Teenagers—Health and hygiene. 2. Body image in adolescence. 3. Beauty, Personal, in children. 4. Surgery, Plastic. I. Title. II. Se-ries.
  RA777.L495 2004
  613'.0433—dc22
                              2004001883

First edition, 2005
13 12 11 10 09 08 07 06 05   10 9 8 7 6 5 4 3

Designed and produced by Harding House Publishing Service, Vestal, NY 13850.
www.hardinghousepages.com
Cover design by Benjamin Stewart.
Printed and bound in Malaysia.

This book is meant to educate and should not be used as an alterna-tive to appropriate medical care. Its creators have made every effort to ensure that the information presented is accurate and up to date—but this book is not intended to substitute for the help and services of trained medical professionals.

CONTENTS

INTRODUCTION

by Dr. Sara Forman

You're not a little kid anymore. When you look in the mirror, you probably see a new person, someone who's taller, bigger, with a face that's starting to look more like an adult's than a child's. And the changes you're experiencing on the inside may be even more intense than the ones you see in the mirror. Your emotions are changing, your attitudes are changing, and even the way you think is changing. Your friends are probably more important to you than they used to be, and you no longer expect your parents to make all your decisions for you. You may be asking more questions and posing more challenges to the adults in your life. You might experiment with new identities—new ways of dressing, hairstyles, ways of talking—as you try to determine just who you really are. Your body is maturing sexually, giving you a whole new set of confusing and exciting feelings. Sorting out what is right and wrong for you may seem overwhelming.

Growth and development during adolescence is a multifaceted process involving every aspect of your being. It all happens so fast that it can be confusing and distressing. But this stage of your life is entirely normal. Every adult in your life made it through adolescence—and you will too.

But what exactly is adolescence? According to the American Heritage Dictionary, adolescence is "the period of physical and psychological development from the onset of puberty to maturity." What does this really mean?

In essence, adolescence is the time in our lives when the needs of childhood give way to the responsibilities of adulthood. According to psychologist Erik Erikson, these years are a time of separation and individuation. In other words, you are separating from your parents, becoming an individual in your own right. These are the years when you begin to make decisions on your own. You are becoming more self-reliant and less dependent on family members.

When medical professionals look at what's happening physically—what they refer to as the biological model—they define the teen years as a period of hormonal transformation toward sexual maturity, as well as a time of peak growth, second only to the growth during the months of infancy. This physical transformation from childhood to adulthood takes place under the influence of society's norms and social pressures; at the same time your body is changing, the people around you are expecting new things from you. This is what makes adolescence such a unique and challenging time.

Being a teenager in North America today is exciting yet stressful. For those who work with teens, whether by parenting them, educating them, or providing services to them, adolescence can be challenging as well. Youth are struggling with many messages from society and the media about how they should behave and who they should be. "Am I normal?" and "How do I fit in?" are often questions with which teens wrestle. They are facing decisions about their health such as how to take care of their bodies, whether to use drugs and alcohol, or whether to have sex.

This series of books on adolescents' health issues provides teens, their parents, their teachers, and all those who work with them accurate information and the tools to keep them safe and healthy. The topics include information about:

- normal growth
- social pressures
- emotional issues
- specific diseases to which adolescents are prone
- stressors facing youth today
- sexuality

The series is a dynamic set of books, which can be shared by youth and the adults who care for them. By providing this information to educate in these areas, these books will help build a foundation for readers so they can begin to work on improving the health and well-being of youth today.

1

Will Everyone Who Likes Their Looks Please Stand Up?

The radio announcer's too-cheery voice blared in Jason's ear. Jason groaned, rolled over, and smacked the clock radio until it fell silent. With one arm bent to shield his eyes from the morning glare, Jason searched in the blankets with his other hand. Finding what he was looking for, he grasped the remote control, turned on the television, and gathered his strength to roll out of bed.

From the flickering screen, another too-cheery person spoke. The Fitness King of morning television was smilingly guiding his viewers through their "No Pain, No Gain" workout. His muscles bulged, rippled, and glistened as he moved effortlessly on the rowing machine. Jason pulled a pair of sweat pants over his skinny legs but didn't let his eyes stray from the television screen. He'd only been awake for two minutes, but already Jason felt terrible.

In the bathroom, Jason brushed his teeth then made a few faces in the mirror. Stepping back, he looked at his chest from different angles. Dissatisfied with what he saw, he flexed his muscles then frowned. His day was getting worse by the moment.

Back in his bedroom, Jason finished dressing while a commercial flashed across the television screen. "Hate the way you look?" a strong voice boomed. "Tired of those skinny legs and flabby arms? Feel like you don't have what it takes? Sick of never having a date? You need a total makeover, and we'll show you how. For a limited time only, for the low price of $39.99, you can get the look women really want."

Feeling worse than ever, Jason turned the television off. He thought the commercial was right. He did need a total makeover, and maybe today he would start. Maybe today he would begin lifting weights, running, eating right, and getting new clothes. Maybe then he'd become the person he truly wanted to be.

Think for a moment about the following statistics. According to studies done by the National Eating Disorders Association, 80 percent of women say they are dissatis-

Many teens are dissatisfied with their bodies.

fied with their bodies. Similarly, 80 percent of ten-year-old children are afraid of being fat. Unhappiness with one's body appears to affect younger children as well. A shocking 42 percent of first and third graders want to be thinner. Statistics like these make a striking statement. They say that an awful lot of people in North America dislike their bodies and wish they could change the way they look.

Jason is not alone in being unhappy with his looks. Who among us wouldn't like to change something about the way we look? In North American culture, beauty is highly valued, and if you are like most people, there are probably parts of your body that you wish could be "bet-

Males as well as females often worry about their physical size and appearance.

ter." Perhaps you would like a less-prominent nose or fuller lips. Maybe you wish your muscles were firmer and your shoulders wider. You might give just about anything to have slightly bigger breasts and slightly smaller hips. If you're like many people, you're willing to try any and every salve, ointment, and cream to make your skin clear and any diet to lose a little weight.

Wanting to have a beautiful body is a perfectly normal desire, and making improvements to your body can be both physically and emotionally healthy. Liking the way you look can help you feel happy, confident, and outgoing. When you feel good about yourself, you walk taller and smile more. When you don't like the way you look, you may feel less confident or even wish that you could hide.

Feeling confident about oneself is incredibly important to a person's self-esteem and ability to succeed, and feeling good about one's physical body can play an important role in building that confidence. However, huge numbers of people today have ***distorted*** views of what a "good" body is. Many people can't feel happy about their bodies because they have an unrealistic view of beauty. Especially in your teen years, when there is so much pressure to look good, it can be surprisingly easy to go too far in the quest for the "perfect" body or look. Many teens set unattainable beauty goals. They expect too much from their own bodies and demand too much of others' bodies. As we will soon see, the results of going too far in our quests for beauty can be damaging and irreversible. For many young people, the way they look becomes an ***obsession***, and unhappiness about the way they look causes low self-esteem and despair.

So if you are a young person who is unhappy with your appearance, what should you do? Perhaps discomfort with your appearance is spilling over into other areas of your life and inhibiting your ability to succeed physically, emotionally, intellectually, or socially. Perhaps you think a makeover, a new you, will make all the difference in the world. Maybe you think that changing your looks will change your life. If this sounds like you, then there are some important things you should consider before taking radical steps to change your appearance.

15

What Is a Makeover—and What Do People Really Want from One?

In North America, makeovers mean big money. Entire industries are based on the idea of makeovers. The average grocery store carries thousands of products that promise to make your skin softer, your hair shinier, your muscles bigger, your thighs firmer, and more. Sitting side-by-side with those products are thousands of books and magazines that promise to reveal the secret of how you can get the perfect body. And who are all these products and publications meant for? Who are these compa-

Many products promise to deliver the perfect body—whatever that is!

16

nies advertising for and trying to woo? If you are a teen in North America, then a large number of these products are meant for you. Makeovers are a multi-billion dollar industry, and to the people who stand to make money from this industry, teenagers who feel insecure about their looks and have a little money to spend are the *cash cow*.

> ### Think You're Not Image Concerned?
>
> Try this: Keep track of the time you devote to image in a day. How much time do you spend in front of the mirror? How many times do you fix your hair? How many commercials do you see that advertise beauty-enhancing products? How many magazines do you read that discuss beauty? Now compare the amount of time you spent focused on image to the amount of time you devoted to things like hobbies, homework, or time spent with your family.

Why are teens such a promising market for the makeover industry? Because the physical and emotional changes that most people go through in their teen years often cause people to feel self-conscious and uncomfortable with their bodies. This discomfort with ourselves pushes us to seek remedies (often on the grocery-store shelves) for our awkward selves. For example, in your teen years, you are probably making more of an effort to alter or improve your body than you did when you were younger. As a kid, you ran and played games for fun without thinking about the health benefits of this exercise.

Can I Change the Way I Look?

Now you might run and play sports for the health, fitness, and toned physique the exercise brings. When you were younger, you wore clothes to cover your body and keep you warm. Now you may spend your mornings wondering what outfit will flatter your body's "good" points and hide your body's "bad" points. Once an outfit is chosen, you may spend the rest of your morning gelling your hair or putting on makeup. As a teen, how your body looks and feels and what other people think of your body is more important than it is for young kids. Add to this mix the cocktail of **hormones** raging through your body and the **tumultuous** emotions they can cause, and you have a recipe for self-esteem disaster.

Feeling awkward in or dissatisfied with your changing body may leave you wishing you could have a total makeover. But what does the word "makeover" mean to you? When a person says she wants a makeover, does she simply want to *improve* the way she looks and feels, or does she want something more? When people use the word makeover, they don't usually mean a simple improvement to the way they look. They usually mean that they want a *whole new* look, something completely different from what they had before. Many people cannot be satisfied with subtle improvements to their bodies. They want their bodies to be reborn with hard muscles, slim hips, runway-model looks, and movie-star hair. Many people who say they want makeovers don't want to look like better versions of themselves. They want to look like a whole new person. But where does this desire come from? Why do we feel driven to have makeovers? Why are the improvements that come with good health not enough? Do we really dislike ourselves so much that we need to completely wipe away the old self in order to get a new one?

18

Body Image: What It Is and How You Got It

Every person has something known as a body image, and this body image plays an important part in that person's life. Your body image is the foundation for how you regard your physical appearance and has a close relationship to how you feel about yourself. Let's take a closer look at body image, what it is, and how it is formed.

Your body image depends only partially on the image you see when you look in the mirror.

19

Can I Change the Way I Look?

Each individual has a picture of himself that he holds in his mind's eye. Furthermore, every person has an idea or belief about how other people see him. These two things form a person's body image. Body image, however, isn't just about how you think your body looks. Body image is about much more than appearance. Your body image also encompasses your beliefs about how your body performs, what you think your body is capable of, and the emotions you feel when you think about your body. Furthermore, your body image is about experience—what it is like to live in your body and how it feels both physically and emotionally to be inside your skin. As you can see, body image is a complicated and ***multifaceted*** concept that incorporates many different aspects of your personal experience.

Your body image doesn't develop overnight. Rather, it is something that develops slowly over time, and many things influence it. For example, years of playing sports and being involved in athletic activities can help build a positive body image by giving a person confidence in her body and its strengths and abilities. On the other hand, hearing one thoughtless or unkind comment about your body can have a long-lasting negative impact on your body image. Furthermore, body image continues to evolve and change throughout your whole life. Most people adjust their body images as they physically, mentally, and emotionally age and mature. You can have a negative body image at one time in your life and a positive body image at another time. Building a positive body image, therefore, is a never-ending process.

It is important to remember that body image does not necessarily have anything to do with the actual appearance or abilities of your body. For many people, body image does not conform to their bodies' physical realities. This is especially true for people who have negative

20

body images. For example, many people see themselves as overweight, when in reality they are not. Some people with strong, athletic bodies truly believe they are weak and incapable. On the other hand, some people see themselves as healthy and slim when their bodies are actually unhealthy and overweight. Distorted body images like these can be a sign of other emotional or psychological issues in a person's life and can have a significant impact on physical and mental health.

> According to a survey done by the magazine *Psychology Today*, many people focus on and criticize individual parts of their bodies. For example, 66 percent of women and 52 percent of men sampled said they were dissatisfied with their weight while 71 percent of women and 63 percent of men were dissatisfied with their abdomens.

Your body image has a large influence on your self-image—the way that you perceive yourself and believe that others perceive you. Your body is clearly an important part of yourself, but it is not the only part of yourself. Things like your mind and your personality traits should also be important parts of your self-image. Understandably, most people have a difficult time imagining themselves separate from their bodies. Having your body image become too large a part of your self-image, however, can create significant problems. If you place too much emphasis on your body and how it looks, you may forget other important and valuable characteristics of yourself. You may also begin to judge others according to

21

their bodies instead of according to the type of person they are. You may not realize how big a role your body plays in determining your sense of self, but think about these questions:

> Do you think you would be the same person if you looked different?
> Do you think people would treat you differently if you looked different?
> Do you think "beautiful" people have an easier time making friends than people who aren't "beautiful"? Do you think the same applies for succeeding in things like school and work?
> Do you feel more confident on a "good-hair day" or a "bad-hair day"?

Make a list of adjectives that you think describe yourself. Now look at your list. Does it consist of physical characteristics (like your height, size, attractiveness, and hair color) or non-physical characteristics (like being funny, smart, mean, or friendly)?

The truth is that many of us in North American society tend to be very body and image oriented. Not all cultures are this way. There are still a few places in the world where a person can go her whole life without ever even seeing her reflection in a mirror. How do you think you would understand and describe yourself if you didn't know what you looked like? What type of body image would you have? What type of self-image would you have?

The teenage years are especially important for the development of body and self-image. It is during these years that you gain more independence as a person. You want to establish yourself as an individual and discover your own unique self. Your body is changing rapidly, propelling you towards physical adulthood. Every physical change in your body can trigger a change in your body image, and maturing towards adulthood makes you think of yourself in a whole new way. Much of this ***maturation*** is positive, and lots of young people look forward to physical changes like getting taller, developing breasts, or having a deeper voice. At the same time, certain stages of this development can leave you feeling awkward and insecure, as if you are walking around in a body that isn't your own. Furthermore, many of the influences that you are exposed to on a daily basis can also make developing a positive body image very difficult and confusing.

These life changes can be uncomfortable, but every adult who is alive today went through them. You might wonder, then, why there isn't more support for teenagers who are feeling uncomfortable with their bodies. Why are so few people telling you that your body is okay and so many people telling you that your body needs to change? Where is this message that you need a makeover coming from?

2

THE BEAUTY TRAP:
Being a Teen in North American Culture

Most people would like to be beautiful, but what is beauty? Does everyone have the same idea of what is beautiful? Is there one image or "look" that is the most beautiful? How do we come to see certain things as beautiful and other things as not beautiful?

There are many things that influence the way you feel about your body and the image you have of beauty. There is no one image of beauty that is the same for everyone everywhere. Beauty is something that is culturally relative, meaning that different cultures around the world have different ideas about what is beautiful and what constitutes an attractive body. In one place, a plump body might be desirable. In another place, people might value a slimmer body. In a certain culture, dark skin may be preferred over light. In another culture, pale skin might be the ideal. In some areas, it is preferable to be very tall. In other areas, height is not an important beauty standard. Furthermore, different cultures perform different ***interventions*** on the body to achieve beauty. In North America, our most common beauty in-

Many young women use makeup to achieve the "look" they desire.

terventions are things like makeup, exercise, and diets, but in other cultures things like scarring and piercing the face are common beauty interventions.

Historically, beauty standards have often been set by the **upper classes** in a society. In many cultures, physical attributes that are associated with wealth also become associated with beauty. For example, in societies that are experiencing famine or lack of food, a plump body (a sign of wealth and strength in an otherwise bleak picture of wasting and emaciation) is often seen as beautiful. In a society that has plenty of food (like North America), thinness becomes associated with wealth because wealthy people have the time and the money to dedicate to things like fitness and special diets. In such a well-fed society, being thin or skinny becomes beautiful. In situations like these, people do not necessarily consciously associate the physical attributes of wealth with beauty, but wealth is desirable, and therefore the physical attributes of wealthy people become desirable. Similarly, in societies where large families consisting of many children are desirable, physical attributes that are associated with fertility, like wide hips and large breasts in women, are also associated with beauty. In societies where few children are desired, these physical signs of fertility may not be considered beautiful. These trends are of course not universal, but there are many examples throughout history of beauty being associated with wealth and good health.

A good way to see how images of beauty have changed throughout time is to look at art. Artwork often portrays *idealized* images of the time period in which the art was created. When you look at paintings depicting Greek gods and goddesses, for example, you may be surprised to see how round and plump the women are. The men also, though well-muscled according to the standards of

27

the time, look "soft" when compared to the images of men we see today. Looking at paintings from the Italian Renaissance, you may be struck by how thin or "puny" the men look by today's standards. Look at the artwork of other cultures as well. What types of differences do you see?

Even if we know the origins of certain ideals of beauty, we still must wonder how those ideals get transmitted throughout an entire culture. How is it that so many people get the same idea of what is beautiful? In North America, the media plays a particularly important role in determining what we consider beautiful and transmitting those ideas throughout the culture.

You've probably heard people talk about "the media" and its influence on popular culture before, but what is the media? The media is made up of all the forms of information transmission in our culture. Therefore, the media consists of things like television, movies, newspapers, magazines, art, books, radio, and the Internet. There is probably no other place in the world where the media is as powerful and as ***accessible*** as it is in North America. One of the reasons for this is ***political***. In North America, the media does not have the same restrictions placed on it that exist in other parts of the world. But another very important reason for the media's power in North America is ***economic***. North American media is made up of numerous multi-billion-dollar industries. Many companies invest huge sums of

Marilyn Monroe, considered by many to be the greatest beauty of her time, was five feet, five and a half inches tall and sometimes wore a size fourteen. Today, the average woman wears a size fourteen but considers herself overweight.

Magazines, television shows, and movies all promote the concept of the "perfect body." However, few women can actually attain the size and shape of models like the young woman pictured above.

money in getting messages out to you, and the popular media is the perfect *forum* for spreading these messages.

A good deal of the messages that are pumped to you through the popular media have to do with selling products that promise to make you more beautiful. But in order to sell you a beauty product, a company must be sure that your ideal or conception of beauty is the same image that the product promises to bestow. For example, if in a certain place, people dislike plump abdomens, then it makes sense for a company to advertise products that promise to reduce the size of a person's abdomen. However, if everyone in a certain place liked plump ab-

Can I Change the Way I Look?

Exercise classes have become a popular trend in today's culture.

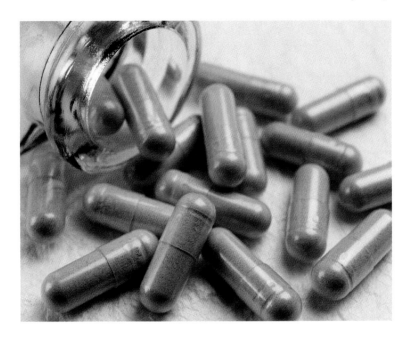

Some medications and herbal remedies promise to deliver a particular body appearance. There are no "miracle pills," however.

domens, it would be ridiculous for a company to try to sell products meant to slim everyone's stomach down because no one would buy the product and the company would lose money.

To be sure that their products are desirable to the population, companies will on the one hand study society for trends and then develop products that are compatible with those trends. On the other hand, however, companies themselves also try to develop trends and to keep profitable trends going by promoting certain ideas over others and trying to get you to believe these ideas are good ones. Companies have many tactics for persuading you into thinking a particular idea, image, or product is a good one and worth spending your money on. Often these tactics consist of using actors, models, sports heroes, and other people who exude images of health, physical strength, and beauty to **endorse** products. Advertisements involving such people imply that by using the product, you can become like the person who is endorsing the product. In the vast majority of cases, however, the famous or beautiful person you see never even used the product they are endorsing before they were offered money to endorse it!

One idea that has proven particularly profitable for companies selling their products in North America is the idea of the makeover. In fact, North Americans spend more than $40 billion dollars each year on image- and beauty-related services and products. But who is it that North Americans are trying to look like? What are they trying to make themselves over as?

Nail polish is just one of many cosmetic products designed to change a person's physical appearance.

Our culture even dictates the shape of our eyebrows!

NORTH AMERICAN WOMEN: BATTLING TO BE THIN

Walk down the checkout aisle at the grocery store. Turn on the television for ten minutes. Flip through a fashion magazine, or look at the advertisements hanging in storefronts. It's pretty clear what a beautiful North American woman is supposed to look like. She's supposed to be tall and thin with perfect skin, voluptuous breasts, and long, flowing hair. But how many people do

The average super model is five feet, eleven inches tall, weighs 117 pounds, wears a size four, and is thinner than 98 percent of American women. The average American woman is five feet, four inches tall and weighs 142 pounds.

you know who actually look like this? The truth is that the female body you see on the front of that fashion magazine is an **unattainable** ideal. You may think that woman is simply blessed with rare **genes**. She probably is, but her beauty secret goes much further than that. She also has the benefit of dieticians, personal trainers, and make-up artists. Her job is to look good, so a huge portion of her time (and a great deal of money) is devoted to developing this image. Even with all of this help, however, this woman will still never look as good walking down the street as she does on the cover of the magazine. That's because her beauty is not just the product of good genes, starvation, hard work, and talented artists. She has also been photographed under special lights and carefully planned conditions. After that photograph was taken, it went through an elaborate design process that included airbrushing and computer enhancement to minimize or eliminate any remaining "flaws" and to "improve" parts of the body. Like so much of what you will read inside that magazine, the picture on its cover is a work of fiction.

It is a sad reality, but the look that so many women struggle so hard to obtain is unrealistic. All over North America, women and girls are starving themselves, exercising religiously, spending huge amounts of money, and hating their bodies for something that only exists in pictures.

North American Men: Bulking Up

Contrary to many people's beliefs, the pressure to be beautiful isn't just on women, and women aren't the only people suffering in their pursuit of the perfect body. If you are a young man in North America, you are being bombarded by images as well, and these images are no more realistic than the images women are faced with.

Like women, boys and men are also told that it is important for them to have clear skin, good hair, and no fat. But there is another body image that boys and men are challenged to live up to. Whereas women are encouraged to become ever smaller in their quest for thinness and femininity, men are challenged to be *masculine*. In our society, being masculine has become *synonymous* with being "big."

> While over the decades Barbie™ has been getting thinner, G.I. Joe™ has been working out, beefing up, and getting buff. In 1964, G.I. Joe™ had a plastic physique that would have translated into a man with a 44-inch chest, 32-inch waist, and 12-inch bicep. A G.I. Joe™ sold in the mid-1990s would have translated into a man with an unbelievable 55-inch chest and 27-inch bicep.

The main image of masculinity that boys and men are confronted with today is an image that many people call the "super-male." This is an image of a man with huge muscles but very little body fat. This man is "ripped" or

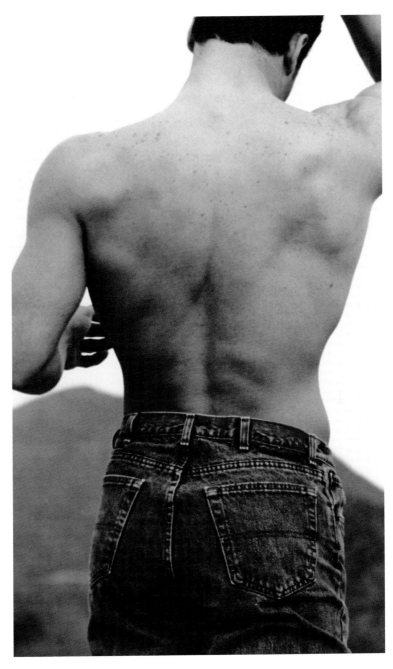

"cut." He has wide shoulders, large pecs, and a thin, tapered waist. His legs are hugely muscular, and his hard body looks like it may have been chiseled out of stone. His entire image exudes strength and masculinity. Simply put, he is huge.

The image of the super-male is portrayed by **gurus** in the fitness industry, by the super-heroes of comic books, by the musclemen of action movies, and in the molded plastic of action figures. Many parents worry about the unrealistic and ultra-feminine images girls are exposed to when playing with Barbie™ dolls. Few parents, however, think about the ultra-masculine images boys are confronted with every time they play with a G.I. Joe™.

Just as with female images of beauty, the images of masculinity that you see splashed on magazine covers, printed on the labels of diet supplements, and hanging on posters at fitness clubs are not realistic images of the human body. Most men don't realize that, no matter how devoted they become to diet and weight lifting, they cannot achieve these body sizes and **musculatures**. Like female models and actors, for most of these super-males, looking good is a fulltime job. Personal trainers, dieticians, make-up artists, and money are all invested in creating these ripped bodies. Male body builders have all of their hair removed by shaving, waxing, or **electrolysis**, and then oil their bodies to make their muscles look harder and more defined. Like images of super models in magazines, the pictures of super-males have also been taken under special conditions, touched up, and enhanced with computer imaging. Furthermore, the super-male image far exceeds what the average human body can achieve. In the vast majority of cases, those who have achieved these hulking forms have done so through unnatural, unsafe, and often illegal means.

The Unattainable Ideal

Today, even movie stars can't obtain our culture's ideals of beauty. Models suffer from eating disorders, actors and athletes take steroids or other muscle-building substances, famous and wealthy people have access to dieticians, personal trainers, professional make-up artists, and plastic surgeons, and still their photographs are airbrushed and digitally enhanced to create the picture of beauty you see every time you go to the grocery store or turn on the television. Despite these facts, however, most people still feel a great deal of dissatisfaction with themselves for not living up to these cultural ideals and wish they could change their bodies. Many of us do a whole variety of small and large things every day in our quest for beauty. Unfortunately, health risks can come with these makeover techniques.

3

More Than Skin Deep:
Cosmetics, Tanning, Tattoos, and More

Gretchen gave an exasperated sigh as her father pounded on the bathroom door for the third time. "Don't rush me!" she called in response to his knocking.

"What on earth are you

doing in there?" her father called back, frustration obvious in his voice. "Other people need to use this bathroom."

"I'm getting ready!" Gretchen yelled as she slammed her mascara on the counter. She stooped down, turned on the water, and left it running to drown her father out.

"Five minutes! Then I'm going in the basement and turning the hot water off!" Her dad responded as he stomped away down the stairs.

They went through this routine every morning. Gretchen rolled her eyes and continued applying her makeup.

Cosmetics and Personal-Care Products

Does the above story sound familiar? How does your day begin? For many people, the start of the day is marked by an elaborate beauty routine. A typical morning may begin with tooth care involving products promising whiter teeth, fresher breath, and a more beautiful smile. Next comes a shower that may include soaps, body-scrubs, shampoos, and conditioners. Then there are the shaving gels, aftershaves, moisturizers, fragrances, hair gels, creams, mousses, and cosmetics.

You may use any number of these products, not only in a makeover attempt, but also in your simple, everyday body care. Most of the products listed above are things that we come in contact with numerous times throughout the day. If you are like most people, you probably assume that if you can buy these prevalent products on

This woman did not wake up looking like this. Cosmetic chemicals gave her this appearance.

grocery-store shelves, they are safe for use on your body. If you are like most people, your thinking is wrong.

According to Kim Erickson, author of *Drop-Dead Gorgeous: Protecting Yourself from the Hidden Dangers of Cosmetics*, each day when we slather our bodies with beauty-enhancing, skin-nourishing, age-defying products, we are also slathering our bodies with potentially dangerous, perhaps even deadly chemicals. According to Erickson, the average person is unknowingly exposed to more than two hundred chemicals every day. The vast majority of these chemicals, even if they are dangerous, will have no immediately observable effect on your body. Much of the danger, however, lies in long-term exposure.

43

Can I Change the Way I Look?

Many women use mascara—but few consider what chemicals they are applying to their eyelashes.

If you are exposed to a tiny bit of a dangerous chemical once, it may not hurt you. But what happens when you are exposed to a tiny bit of this chemical day after day? What if this chemical is in a shampoo that washes over your head and body every morning? What if it is in the moisturizer you rub into your skin twice a day? What if it is in the lipstick you spread on your lips every few hours? And perhaps most importantly, how can a **toxic** chemical be approved for use on your body?

The answer to this question lies largely in the *amount* of toxic chemical in any given product. Just because a product has been proven to cause cancer, interrupt hormones, or alter **DNA** (as many chemicals used in cosmetics have) doesn't mean that chemical can't be used in a cosmetic product. Sometimes it just means that the chemical can only be used in small, specified amounts. Research and safety studies have shown that small amounts of these chemicals, though they may cause allergic reactions in some people, will not cause immediate harm to most people. What we do not know, in most cases, is what the long-term effects of repeated exposure to these chemicals will be. If you use many of these products on a daily basis, or if you are considering purchasing new products to help make yourself over, you should investigate these products' ingredients and potential health risks.

The number-one health risk of cosmetics and personal care products is allergic reaction. Allergic reactions are extremely common and often occur in response to the fragrances used in these products. Allergic reactions can range from mild skin irritation to severe pain, burning, blistering, or peeling skin, irritated eyes, sinus **infections**, asthma attacks, nausea, vomiting, and other reactions. If you are trying a new beauty product for the first time, you should first perform an allergy test to see if the product will be safe for you. Many products, like hair dyes and ***depilatory*** creams, have instructions for performing allergy tests. If the product you wish to try, however, has no instructions, you can usually perform an adequate test by putting a small amount of the product on the sensitive skin on the inside of your forearm (the area of your arm between your wrist and your elbow). Let twenty-four hours pass. If within twenty-four hours you see a rash, redness, swelling or other sign of reaction, you should not use the product.

Allergic reactions, however, are not the only risk that comes with beauty products. Other risks include cancer, disruption of hormones, interference in ***neurological*** activity, and weakening of the ***immune system***.

Of the hundreds of potentially dangerous chemicals that can be found in the cabinets of your bathroom, Erickson names nine that are particularly dangerous. She calls these the "Nine Deadly Ingredients." They are listed in the following order in her book:

Coal tar colors. All FD&C and D&C colors are made from a poisonous tar found in bituminous coal. These colors are listed on ingredients labels according to the following format: FD&C or D&C, their color, and their number— for example: FD&C Yellow No. 5. Many of these colors have been banned from use in food products because of their ***carcinogenic***, or cancer-causing, properties. But in the case of these artificial colors, a specific color is only banned from use after it has been proven to be unsafe. Coal tar colors that have not undergone safety testing, therefore, can still be put in foods and cosmetics even when we don't know the dangers they may pose. Whether a specific FD&C or D&C color has been proven unsafe or not, it is important for you to remember that all coal tar colors come from the same basic ingredients and should therefore be regarded as potentially carcinogenic.

Formaldehyde. Formaldehyde is a preservative that can damage DNA and cause lung cancer. Perhaps you've run across formaldehyde in science or biology classes where it may be used to preserve the dead bodies of frogs or pigs you will dissect in your lessons. In cosmetics, this chemical is added to kill germs and fungus and to preserve the cosmetic. Even though formaldehyde is very common in cosmetics, you probably will not see it listed on the ingredients label. That is because formaldehyde is rarely added as a pure ingredient. Instead, it exists in cosmetics as an ingredient within an ingredient. For example, on your shampoo bottle, you may not see formaldehyde listed by name, but you may very well see DMDM Hydantoin, which is a toxic preservative, 17.7 percent of which is formaldehyde. Another common ingredient that often contains formaldehyde is sodium lauryl sulfate, which is found in 90 percent of shampoos. Believe it or not, if you know how to look, you can find formaldehyde in everything from nail polish to toothpaste.

> According to the National Institute of Occupational Safety and Health, 884 of the approximately 5500 chemicals approved for use in cosmetics are toxic.

Lead. Lead is the third ingredient on Erickson's deadly list, but Erickson is certainly not the first person to realize the dangers of lead. For years, we have known that lead exposure can cause problems ranging from neuro-

Even so-called safe cosmetics can cause allergic reactions.

logical disorders, to mental retardation, to death. Nevertheless, small amounts of lead can still be found in cosmetics and personal care products, specifically in certain hair dyes. Like other dangerous substances, an extremely small amount of lead may not have an immediate negative effect on your body. The problem with lead, however, is that once it is in your body, it does not leave. Lead particles can be ingested, inhaled, or absorbed through the skin. Once in your body, the lead gets stored in your body tissues. The more lead you are exposed to, the more lead you will have in your body and the greater your level of poisoning will become. The **cumulative** effects of lead buildup in the body can be devastating and even deadly.

Nitrosamines. Nitrosamines are another type of carcinogenic chemical that can be found in cosmetics, especially in shampoos. Unlike some of the other chemicals we have discussed, nitrosamines are not intentionally added to cosmetics. Instead, they occur as **by-products** resulting from the mixing of other chemicals. Chemicals that can produce nitrosamines when mixed with other chemicals include monoethanolamine, diethanolamine, and triethanolamine. These chemicals are often listed in ingredients labels as MEA, DEA, and TEA. Other chemicals that can produce nitrosamines are formaldehyde and sodium lauryl sulfate.

Phenylenediamine. This chemical can also be absorbed through the skin and can cause various forms of skin irritation, asthma, and other serious conditions. Recent studies have shown 4-Chloro-o-phenylenediamine to be a probable human carcinogen. It was originally patented for use in hair dyes. Today, phenylenediamine or other similar substances are used in multiple industries, dyes, and products containing dyes. Some ingredients that may contain phenylenediamine or its components include paraphenylenediamine (PPD or PPDA), 1,4-Benzenediamine, 1,4-Penylenediamine, Rodol™ D, Para-aminoaniline (p-aminoaniline), Orsin™, Ursol™, and Paradiaminobenzene (p-diaminobenzene). Some forms of the chemical are regulated in the United States by the **Environmental Protection Agency** under the Toxic Substances Control Act and by the Occupational Safety and

Health Administration under the Hazard Communication Standard.

Propylene glycol. This chemical is a common ingredient in moisturizers and moisturizing cosmetics. Propylene glycol is classified by the **U.S. Food and Drug Administration** as "generally recognized as safe," but studies suggest it may interfere with neurological function and might damage your skin cells, kidneys, and liver. Though it may make your skin feel soft at first, many people will experience irritation or allergic reaction when repeatedly using a product containing propylene glycol.

Quaternary ammonium compounds. These compounds are used in cosmetics to soften skin, preserve the cosmetic, and kill germs, among other uses. Unfortunately, quaternary ammonium compounds can also be toxic and can irritate the delicate tissues of your skin and eyes. Skin reactions can range from mild irritation to severe burns depending on the amount of the chemical and the sensitivity of your skin. Some quaternary ammonium compounds you may find listed in your cosmetics are benzalkonium chloride, cetrimonium bromide, and quaternium 1-29.

Sodium lauryl sulfate. If you're like many people, you probably enjoy the thick, rich lather of a shampoo, soap, or body-wash. Commercials for these products often show mounds of glistening white bubbles washing luxuriously over soft skin. This foaming quality so highly valued in our personal care products, however, does not result from the products' cleansing properties. Instead, sodium lauryl sulfate (sometimes called sodium laureth sulfate) is added to 90 percent of shampoos to give them this rich lather. Sodium lauryl sulfate, however, can dam-

Many hair products contain chemicals that are potentially harmful.

age your skin cells and cause allergic reactions as well as combine with other chemicals to form nitrosamines. Furthermore, shampoos are not the only cosmetic or cleansing products that contain sodium lauryl sulfate. This chemical can also be found in some skin creams, soaps, body-washes, and toothpastes.

Talc. Number nine on Erickson's list, talc is another potentially dangerous chemical that is commonly found in our bathroom cabinets. This may surprise you since talcum powder or powders containing talc are very commonly applied to babies' skin to reduce the moisture that causes diaper rash. People often use talcum powder after showering or on a hot summer day to reduce moisture

The foaming qualities of many products are caused by sodium lauryl sulfate.

and stickiness. Talc is similar in its chemical composition to asbestos, a material that was formerly used as a fire **re-tardant** in buildings. Today, we know that inhaling asbestos fibers can cause lung cancer and other health problems. Similarly, inhaling particles of talcum powder has been shown to cause irritation and other problems in the lungs as well as vomiting. Studies have also shown that when women use talcum powder on a regular basis on the genital area, they can increase their risk of developing ovarian cancer by as much as 33 percent. Many cosmetics, including powder-based cosmetics like eyeshadow and blush and liquid cosmetics like foundation, contain talc. Some doctors now suggest, if you want the benefits of powder without the risks of talc, try powdering your skin with cornstarch instead.

The chemicals used in cosmetics are not the only chemicals you need be concerned with when considering the health risks of personal-care products. You should also be aware of the fact that the packaging these products come in can **leach** dangerous chemicals into the air you breathe and into the products you use on your face, skin, and body. This leaching process is often called off-gassing, and it is of special concern with plastics, which are petroleum-based products. Products made from petroleum can contain many carcinogenic and hormone-interrupting chemicals. Some chemicals that leach from packaging can mix with chemicals in cosmetics to create even more dangerous substances.

All of this is not to say that you should be frightened of personal-care products and completely give up things like shampoo, moisturizers, and cosmetics. Many of these products are perfectly safe, and cosmetics, like foods and drugs, are regulated by the Food and Drug Administration (FDA) in the United States and by Health

Canada in Canada. However, cosmetics are not as high of a priority for regulation and safety as foods and drugs, and most of the tests done to determine the safety and quality of these products are done by the companies that make and sell them, companies that will financially benefit from their sale, rather than by independent scientific researchers. This discussion is simply meant to alert you to the fact that just because a product is sold in a grocery or drug store does not mean it is absolutely safe. Many products meant for use on our bodies do contain potentially dangerous ingredients, and you should be aware of this fact so that you can identify these ingredients and protect yourself from health risks. Furthermore, the more of these products that you use, the more you increase your risk of an allergic reaction or other unfortunate health consequence. When applying chemicals to your body, less is more and education is key. When trying new products, always read the ingredients and perform an allergy test before attempting to make yourself over.

Tanning: Aging Beauty

Another popular beauty intervention is tanning. In the mid-1900s, people tanned without understanding the huge health-risks that they faced. Today, however, we understand the extreme damage *UV* rays cause to the skin, the risk of skin cancer and death, and the aging properties of the sun. Nevertheless, shocking numbers of young people flock, not only to the sunny beach, but also to tanning booths to bake beneath deadly rays.

Tanning for beauty when you are young will, without doubt, make you look prematurely old. Your skin will age

The moisturizers in bubblebaths may contain quaternary ammonium compounds.

quickly and wrinkle. It will become dry, leathery, and spotted. If you tan, the DNA in your skin cells *will* change and cancer cells *will* grow. If you are one of those people who thinks, "That will never happen to me," you're wrong. All people have cancer cells develop in their bodies, especially in their skin as it ages and damage *accumulates*. Usually the immune system recognizes and kills the cells before they get out of control. The more damage that has been done to your body, however, and the more cancer cells are forming, the greater the risk that something will get past your immune system. If your

According to some doctors, as much as 90 percent of the wrinkles, sagging, and discoloration on a person's face is due to sun damage rather than to age.

immune system cannot recognize and destroy these cancer cells quickly enough, you will risk disfigurement and death. According to one study, tanning more than once a month increases your risk of developing skin cancer by more than 50 percent. Furthermore, the negative effects of sun damage are not only skin deep. Damage from the sun can also trigger harmful reactions in your immune system.

In today's changing climate and beauty-obsessed culture, the risk of UV exposure cannot be overstated. Too many people, regardless of being educated about the risks of tanning, ignore the warnings and willingly harm their bodies. The truth is, there is NO safe way to tan. Any UV exposure is harmful exposure.

Despite the damage the sun will do to your skin, some exposure to the sun is necessary to initiate the production of vitamin D within your body. Research has also shown that lack of sunlight can play a role in causing or worsening depression. Furthermore, what kind of life would you have if you could never go out in the sun? So what should you do? How can you get the sun you need to stay healthy and happy without making your skin unhealthy?

First of all, every time you go outside, you

Approximately one million people will be diagnosed with skin cancer in the United States this year. Women under the age of forty are the fastest-growing group of skin-cancer patients.

Our culture values suntans—but the sun can damage our skin, causing premature aging and even cancer.

should be wearing a sunscreen that blocks both UVA and UVB rays. Your sunscreen should be applied liberally, and just because you are wearing sunscreen doesn't mean that you can now bake in the sun for hours without damaging your skin. Some scientists believe that operating under the myth that sunscreen completely protects one from sun damage leads some people to stay out in the sun longer and actually increase their risk of developing skin cancer. Even when wearing sunscreen, you should limit your direct exposure to the sun to less than half an hour each day. When out in the sun, wear a protective wide-brimmed hat. Make sure your face, neck, and shoulders are shaded, and avoid the mid-day hours when the sun is at its strongest (generally between eleven in the morning and two in the afternoon). You should also never tan in tanning booths. Natural sunlight is made up of many types of light waves. Tanning booths, however, use higher concentrations of damaging UVA rays to brown your skin. If you absolutely must have that bronze tan for a special occasion, do what so many of today's stars do—get it out of a bottle.

Tattooing, Body Piercing, and Scarification

For thousands of years, human beings have used tattooing, body piercing, and **scarification** to enhance their beauty, mark important life events, participate in cultural ceremonies, and bring one closer to one's god. In North American society today, tattoos and body piercings are still used as markings of beauty and identity. Furthermore, as North American knowledge of, contact with, and respect for other cultures grows, scarification is also increasingly seen in our society.

The decision to permanently alter one's body with a tattoo, body piercing, or intentional scar is often related to a change in a person's identity or a rite of passage. Even in our largely **secular** North American culture, people still use tattoos and body piercings as a physical representation of inner growth. Many people decide to make such alterations to their bodies when they turn eighteen. These bodily alterations often commemorate the person's newly recognized adulthood. People also get such body alterations to mark important life events like falling in love, breaking up, losing a loved one, or experiencing some form of personal triumph. On the other hand, one may decide to get a tattoo, body piercing, or scar because they simply like the way such body alterations look.

In most of North America, you cannot get a tattoo, body piercing, or professional scarification unless you are at least eighteen years old. If younger than this, you need the signed consent of a parent or legal guardian. After you are eighteen, only you can decide what is best for your body. If you decide to have one of these body-altering procedures, you should understand your motivations and be educated about all of the possible benefits and risks before making a decision.

The first thing you should consider when thinking about tattooing, piercing, or scarification is what do you hope to gain or accomplish by altering your body? Having a clear understanding of your desires and motivations is important to minimizing the risk of disappointment and regrets. If, for example, you have always thought nose piercings were very beautiful and wanted one for years, you may be very happy with the results of such a piercing. If, however, you think having such a piercing will make you look tough or cool and will cause people to treat you differently, you may be sorely disappointed when, after your piercing, nothing in your life changes. Knowing why you want your body altered, having realistic hopes for the alteration, and having a clear view of how this alteration will affect your body image are keys to the successful outcome of such an alteration.

If you decide you do wish to alter your body in such a way, the next thing to concern yourself with is safety. Tattoos, body piercings, and scarification each pose certain health risks, and you must know what these risks are to protect yourself. If you are interested in getting a tattoo, piercing, or intentional scar, the first thing you must be aware of is the health risk of dirty needles and unsanitary equipment. Never get a tattoo, piercing, or scar from someone who is not a licensed artist, and never try to perform one of these procedures on yourself or someone else. If you are receiving such a procedure outside of a clean, professional, licensed facility, you greatly increase your risk of being exposed to dirty needles and unsanitary conditions. Such needles can transmit diseases like **HIV**, the virus that causes **AIDS**, and Hepatitis C, a potentially deadly disease that attacks the liver.

When considering one of these body-altering procedures, check out several different licensed facilities. Compare the artistic work, sanitary conditions, experience, and educational materials of the facilities. Have a consultation with the artist so that you can discuss your desires and see the artist's past work. Set your appointment date for at least a week after the consultation so you have time to think over your decision, the design, and how you feel about the artist's work. Ask a local health professional about the safety of the procedure you are considering and the facility you have chosen to perform it. If a certain facility has had many cases of infection or

Tattoos are a permanent way of altering one's body.

other medical complications in the past, a local health professional will be likely to know and able to inform you of any possible risks. If you are considering a tattoo, remember that the tattoo will become a permanent part of your body. Though *laser* removal is sometimes possible, it is both painful and expensive. If you are convincing yourself by saying you can always have the tattoo removed later, you probably shouldn't be getting a tattoo. If you are considering a piercing, keep in mind that even if you later decide to remove the piece of jewelry, you will always have a scar. Similarly, though laser and other plastic surgery procedures can minimize some scars, you will more than likely always have the scar that results from scarification. You should only go through with these procedures if you are sure that you want a permanent change to your body.

Piercing is another common form of body enhancement.

If you do decide to get a tattoo or piercing, make sure that the artist opens a new package of needles in front of you so that you can be assured of cleanliness. Some artists sterilize and reuse equipment. To be properly sterilized, such equipment must be heated to 250 degrees Fahrenheit (121 degrees Centigrade) for thirty minutes. Never accept such a piece of tattooing or piercing equipment unless you can be sure of the sterilization method and its effectiveness. Tattoo artists also sometimes prick their hand to make sure a needle is sharp enough before beginning a tattoo. Be sure that your artist does not do this as any illness that the artist might have could be spread to you.

Needles are not the only risk factor when it comes to transmission of disease. In tattooing, for example, ink can also spread disease. When giving a tattoo, the artist dips the needle into ink, injects the ink into your arm, then returns the needle to gather more ink. In this way, blood and tissue is transported back and forth by way of the needle. To avoid contamination, ink should be poured from its clean bottle into a clean, disposable container used for the tattoo. The ink used for a tattoo should be thrown out immediately after use. Never allow a tattoo to proceed if you are not sure that both the needle and the inks are new and clean.

Other things to consider when thinking about getting a tattoo, piercing, or scar are the risks of infection and allergic reaction. All three of these procedures pose significant infection risks. A serious infection could lead to extensive scarring, even disfigurement. If, after receiving one of these procedures, you have large amounts of puss, pain, redness, swelling, or notice a bad smell coming from the affected area, see a doctor immediately. Tattoos and jewelry in piercings also commonly cause allergic reactions. Some people are allergic to the ink in tattoos.

Such an allergy can be crippling for once the ink is in your skin you cannot easily get rid of it and can never find relief from the allergy. Many people also have allergic reactions to certain metals in the jewelry worn in piercings. To minimize the risk of allergic reaction, you should wear stainless steel jewelry.

CLOTHING

Did you know that even the clothing you wear can pose certain risks to your health? It's true. Natural fibers like cotton, wool, linen, and silk are rarely harmful. Today, however, little clothing is made from 100 percent-pure, natural fibers. Many fabrics are made from **synthetic** fibers, and these fibers are derived from chemicals like petroleum products. Whenever you wear a piece of clothing, tiny particles of the fabric break off onto your skin and into the air. It is quite common for people with sensitive skin or allergies to have allergic reactions to synthetic fibers.

Even if synthetic fibers don't bother you, or your clothing is made of all natural fibers, the dyes in clothing can still cause allergic reactions and other health risks. Like the chemicals in cosmetics, chemicals used to dye clothing can be harmful.

Generally speaking, however, the biggest health risk that clothing poses is to the health of your pocketbook. Trendy, fashionable, or designer clothing can make you feel good, but it can also be a financial burden. One might like to be stylish, but styles change so quickly, how can anyone keep up? Few people can afford to make over their entire wardrobe for every trend and change of season. One can dress nicely without spending tons of money to have all of the latest fashions. Many young people prefer to find, alter, make, and wear clothing that expresses their own individual style rather than simply following trends. Before giving yourself a makeover with a whole new wardrobe, you might want to think about why the style of your clothing is important to you and check the price tag.

It's not wrong to want to enhance or improve your physical appearance. But looking attractive should not cost your health. Find the look that's right for you while educating yourself on the risks and safety precautions that may go along with your appearance goal. Make your decisions based on what's truly best for you. As you become an adult, looking good should go hand-in-hand with accepting and caring for yourself.

4

FOR HEALTH OR FOR BEAUTY:
Makeover Risks in Diet and Exercise

All of us have heard the benefits of a good diet and a healthy exercise program. Being overweight causes health problems and may even shorten your life—while regular exercise and the right diet may actually extend your life. But in

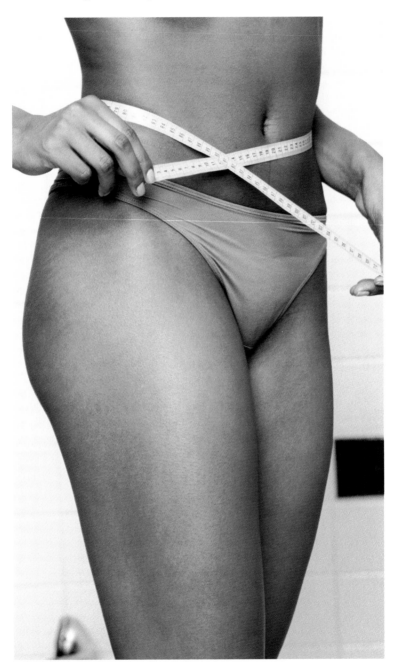

the quest to achieve "perfection," some people take otherwise healthy goals to unhealthy extremes.

Diet and Dieting

For many people, deciding it's time for a makeover is synonymous with deciding it's time to lose weight. Studies show that obesity in North America is on the rise. As obesity rates rise, health conditions like *Type II diabetes* and heart disease also increase. For many North Americans, even many young people, losing weight would be a good idea. But because many people have such distorted views of what is beautiful, there are lots of people who feel they need to be thinner when it wouldn't be healthy for them to lose weight. Furthermore, even if a person's health could benefit from a weight loss, losing weight can still pose health risks if you go about it the wrong way.

When most people think about losing weight, they think about going on a diet. There is a big difference, however, between having a healthy *diet* and *dieting*. The first thing you should know about diets is that they don't work. More than 75 percent of all people who lose weight on a diet will gain that weight back within one year. After five years, 97 percent of people will have gained back all of the weight. Often people who go on diets gain back not only the weight they lost, but additional pounds that they did not bargain for. Furthermore, crash diets and diets that focus on eating just one type of food can be very unhealthy, even dangerous. Such diets limit your nutrients and starve your body of the energy and building blocks that it needs. In addition to starving your body of the nutrients it needs, some diets, like high-protein/low-*carbo-*

hydrate diets, give you too much of certain nutrients, a situation that can have health risks of its own.

High-protein/low-carbohydrate diets, like the famous Atkins diet, are the most popular crash diets today. According to these diets, a person is supposed to eat high-protein and even high-fat foods like eggs, steaks, and hamburger, but little or no carbohydrates, like bread, beans, and rice. Carbohydrates typically make up sixty percent or more of a person's diet, so cutting them out can cause a person to lose weight. However, when you rob your body of carbohydrates, you also rob your body of needed energy and nutrients. Furthermore, when you increase your intake of animal fats and proteins, nutrients that we should typically have in moderation, you also increase your chances of having high cholesterol, heart disease, kidney damage, inflammation of the joints, bad breath and body odor, certain forms of cancer, and numerous other unpleasant side effects.

There are other fad diets that promote different extremes like eating all carbohydrates and no fats or eating just one type of food. In this category, there are things like the all-broccoli diet, the cabbage-soup diet, the grapefruit diet, and all-liquid diets. All of these diets could cause you to lose weight, but none of them would make you healthier.

Diets can be particularly harmful to young people. When you are young, your body is still growing. You need many nutrients, including fats, to keep your body healthy and developing normally. **Overzealous** dieting can lead to **malnutrition**. When you are malnourished, your body and brain work slower and side effects like a slow **metabolism**, dizziness, fatigue, headaches, mood swings, loss of hair, and more begin to result. Calorie and nutrition restriction can stop a woman's menstruation, cause muscle loss, weaken bones, and delay puberty in

A nourishing, well-balanced diet is essential to long-term health.

young people. Most of these effects will end when a person returns to a healthy diet, but long-term calorie and nutrition restriction can cause permanent damage, especially to organs like your heart and kidneys.

Dieting is bad enough for your body, but you face even greater dangers if you turn to diet pills for weight loss. Studies have shown many such pills to be unsafe. As a result, diet pills containing the combination phentermine/fenfluramine (called phen/fen for short) or ephedrine have been withdrawn from the market. These once-common ingredients in diet pills have been linked to heart damage and to some deaths. However, many other diet pills that carry substantial health risks remain available to consumers. Many diet pills rely on excessive doses of caffeine to stimulate the metabolism. Side effects of these diet pills can include irregular heartbeat, dizziness, seizures, high **blood pressure**, addiction, and more.

Instead of dieting or using diet pills, you should be striving to eat and live healthfully every day. A healthy diet is high in vegetables, fruits, complex carbohydrates (like whole wheat, brown rice, and beans), polyunsaturated fats (like extra-virgin olive oil), and proteins. At the same time, it is low in sugar, simple carbohydrates (like white bread, white rice, and white flour pasta), and **saturated**, **hydrogenated**, and **trans fats**. For the vast majority of people, simply eating healthfully every day goes farther in maintaining a healthy weight than diets could ever go.

Exercise is good for you—but you should be careful not to damage your joints by exercising too much or without the proper footware.

EXERCISE

When a person wishes to make herself over by losing weight, exercise is a natural companion to dieting. Exercise is essential to maintaining a healthy body and mind, and no one would contest

> At any given time, one in every three American women and one in every five American men are on some form of diet. Almost none of them will permanently lose weight.

the health benefits of exercise. A person will almost certainly lose more weight with a combination of healthy diet and exercise than with just healthy diet alone, but just as there are safe and unsafe ways of managing your diet, there are also safe and unsafe ways to exercise.

When you exercise, you should never push your body beyond the limits of what is comfortable. Contrary to popular belief, exercise should not be painful. If you are out of shape, you will of course feel some mild discomfort, like getting winded quickly or having slightly sore muscles the next day, but any significant discomfort means you are pushing your body too hard. Strength and endurance need to be built over time, not in one day or one exercise session. Pushing your body too far too fast can cause serious and long-lasting damage.

The most common damage from excessive physical activity is musculoskeletal, meaning it occurs in the muscles and bones. Exercise- and sport-related injuries are especially common to the joints. Joints like your ankles, knees, hips, elbows, and shoulders have to withstand pressure and impacts during exercise. The soft tissues and cartilage in these joints can be easily damaged by high-impact activities like running and playing certain sports. Damage to your joints may increase your risk of

Can I Change the Way I Look?

Exercise is one of the best things you can do for your heart.

developing arthritis, a painful condition of stiffness and *inflammation* of the joints.

Injuries to the muscles are also common, especially when people fail to stretch and warm their muscles before moving into high-impact or aerobic activities. People also often push their bodies too far while playing competitive and contact sports. While in the heat of competition, your mind may tune out the pain your body is feeling. When the game is over, however, you can find that you've done real damage. In extreme cases, as in marathon runners and some professional athletes, excessive exercise can even cause bone fractures, loss of menstruation in women, and contribute to *osteoporosis*.

Exercise is one of the best things you can do for the strength of your heart, but if you have certain conditions, exercise can also put your heart at risk. These risks are far more common in older people rather than in young people, but in rare cases, a young person can have a heart condition that makes exercise more complicated. If you have a previously diagnosed heart condition, you should always check with your doctor before beginning an exercise routine. If you don't have a previously identified condition, but notice extreme and abnormal fatigue, irregular heartbeat, pain localized in your chest or radiating to your left arm, back, throat, or stomach, or dizziness during or after exercise, you should consult with your doctor before continuing with the activity.

If you exercise correctly, however, the risks of exercise are extremely low and far outweighed by the health benefits. Exercise is absolutely essential to good health. You may never look like a supermodel or super male, but twenty minutes of exercise every day can make over your body and mind by making you healthier, happier, and more energetic. To minimize the risks that can come with exercise, do not push your body beyond what you are currently capable of. Start slow and build your routine up slowly over time. This is especially important if you were previously **sedentary**. The risks of injury are the highest when you are just beginning to exercise after a long period of being out of shape. If you are just beginning to exercise, you may want to start with a low-impact activity like walking, swimming, yoga, or water **aerobics** rather than a high-impact activity like running or land aerobics. Additionally, always remember to stretch and warm up before exercising and to end exercise with warming down and another round of stretching. If you do injure yourself, make sure you give your body an adequate recovery period before going back to your exercise routine, and then ease yourself back into the routine slowly.

Bodybuilding, Powerlifting, and Protein Supplements

Men's desires for big, strong muscles are nothing new. What is new, however, is the definition or standard for "big" and "strong" that many people now use—what we previously called the super male. What's also new is the growing number of adolescent and teenage boys who are willing to spend huge amounts of time and money pursuing the super male image. Some men desire the impossible super male image so much that they begin to engage in risky behaviors, like improper bodybuilding, powerlifting, and taking dangerous supplements, in pursuit of this unattainable ideal. The worst part is, however, that many people don't even realize that these behaviors can be risky.

76

Lifting weights, though not an aerobic exercise that significantly strengthens your heart and fitness level, can be great for toning and firming muscles. Many people find that stubborn "soft" areas that just won't go away with regular exercise do become firmer when targeted with weight training. Weight training and the strength that comes with it can also be good for a person's confidence and self-esteem. However, as with everything else we have discussed, there are healthy and unhealthy approaches to training with weights. Unfortunately, many young people, especially many young men, go about weight lifting in the riskiest of ways.

For many weight lifters, the goal of their training is not simply to tone up, but to lift the heaviest weights possible. Lifting heavy weights, however, can be dangerous, especially for people whose bodies are still growing. There is scientific evidence suggesting that lifting heavy weights before you have reached your full height can

damage your growth plates, leading to stunted development. Lifting heavy weights can also cause bone fractures, muscle strain and tearing, and damage to the delicate joints. When you are young and your body is still growing, you are especially susceptible to these types of injuries. For young people, exercise using light to moderate amounts of weight is usually not damaging, but most doctors recommend that young people hold off on the heavy weights used for bodybuilding until they have reached their full height and their bones have stopped growing. This usually happens between the ages of sixteen and eighteen. Nevertheless, with North American society's emphasis on sports, many young people, especially young men, begin bodybuilding while still in high school. They do this to become more competitive in sports where size and weight are an advantage, like American football, hockey, and wrestling. Despite young people's coaches' and even parents' desires for competitiveness in sports, the fact remains that most young men's bodies are not done growing, and therefore not prepared for bodybuilding, until after they graduate from high school.

Thus far we have limited our discussion of weight training and bodybuilding to men. This is not because women don't weight train. In fact, as women begin to see the benefits such training can have for toning and firming their bodies, women are weight training in ever-increasing numbers. However, in North American society it is not generally considered beautiful for a woman to have big muscles, and few women engage in the "hardcore" bodybuilding and powerlifting that increasing numbers of men engage in. There are, however, female bodybuilders, and these women face the same risks of injury that male bodybuilders face.

Can I Change the Way I Look?

There are some additional, important points to consider when thinking about weight training, bodybuilding, and health risks. One is that the need for perfect form and technique increases as the amount of weight increases. If someone is doing an exercise incorrectly with a small amount of weight, he may not gain the full benefits of the exercise, but he is also less likely to injure himself. Doing the exercise improperly with heavy weights is much more likely to cause serious injury. When a person begins a bodybuilding program, he should have a coach, trainer, or other professional available to help him learn proper technique. Unfortunately, many young people dive into the process without professional consultation and adequate training. Some doctors are also beginning to recommend that people considering bodybuilding have their heart and **aorta** checked by a doctor. This is due to the fact that lifting heavy weights causes sudden spikes in blood pressure, and these spikes have recently been linked to a number of cases in which weight lifter's aortas literally ripped open while training. In light of new cases, some doctors think this type of injury may be far more common than previously believed.

Another important point to remember is that many weight-lifting injuries are caused not just by pushing one's body beyond what it can tolerate, but also by losing control of the heavy weights. A lifter should always have a spotter, someone who is standing by ready to help if a person buckles under the strain of weights or if the weights slip. Some people prefer to workout alone, but weight training is an activity that should always be done in groups of at least two. The necessity of working out with other people can make weight training a very social activity, and many people enjoy this aspect of the sport.

Another risky activity that young people seeking large muscles are increasingly engaging in is the practice of

When lifting weights, the proper technique is important for safety.

taking protein or "nutritional" supplements to help build muscle. Creatine is by far the most popular of these substances, and does in fact appear to help athletes get both bigger and stronger. However, creatine and supplements like it can have damaging side effects, and no person should take such a supplement without first discussing the pros and cons with a doctor.

Creatine is a substance that exists in all vertebrates as a natural result of the processing of protein in the body. Creatine appears to play a key role in keeping muscles supplied with energy, and studies and the experiences of thousands of athletes seem to suggest that dietary supplements of creatine can increase athletic performance. However, this increase in athletic performance may not be without negative consequences.

The United States Food and Drug Administration does not regulate nutritional supplements like creatine, so the safety, purity, and *efficacy* of such a product cannot be guaranteed. Furthermore, creatine supplements, though studied more than some other nutritional supplements, have not been studied enough by the scientific community to determine exactly what amounts, if any, are safe for athletes, who should and should not take creatine, and what the long-term side effects of creatine use might be. Some risks, however, are already known. Some of these risks include water retention, weight gain, bloating and diarrhea, nausea, muscle cramps, and seizures. Creatine and protein supplements can also permanently damage your kidneys. Because of the largely unknown health risks, most doctors recommend that people under eighteen, women

Recent studies have found creatine use in children as young as sixth grade.

who are pregnant or nursing, and people with medical conditions of the kidneys do not take creatine.

In these last two chapters, we have surveyed some of the most common techniques and products that people use every day in their quests for beauty and the perfect look. When a person decides it's time for a makeover, cosmetics, diet, exercise, new clothes, lifting weights, and the other topics we discussed are some of the first avenues she might try. However, none of these avenues is without health risks. Some of these health risks are larger than others, but all are worth considering before pursuing a makeover. For most people, the quest for beauty will never take them beyond the steps described in this chapter. Most people who are unhappy with their looks eventually find a resolution, either by accepting their body as it is, or by employing one of the options described above. For other people, however, even these interventions in their looks will not be enough. There are young people today who are engaged in an emotional crisis when it comes to their body image. A crisis of body image can in rare cases even lead to psychiatric illness, and the more severe the crisis of body image, the further people are willing to go in their pursuit of beauty.

5

BODY OBSESSIONS:

Teens in Crisis

Most people do at least a few things every day to increase their attractiveness or improve their looks, but for some people, looks become an obsession. When the way you look becomes an obsession, you may cease to understand what your body truly looks like and begin taking dangerous steps in an attempt to improve your looks. Sometimes, a person's obsession with a body part that he **perceives** as flawed can become so severe that it actually becomes a psychiatric disorder. When people suffer from one of these disorders, a makeover will not help them to feel better about their bodies or themselves and could even complicate their conditions by masking the true problems they must face.

Body Dysmorphic Disorder

At one time or another almost everyone feels some dissatisfaction with at least one part of her body. For a period of time, that body part may occupy the person's thoughts, cause worry, and trigger unhappiness. A person with a healthy body image and a healthy self-image, however, will eventually come to accept the body part that she had previously regarded as flawed. When you have a healthy body image, you realize that everyone's body is different, no one's body is perfect, and in fact the things that make a person's body different can be part of a person's beauty.

Sometimes, however, a person cannot accept a part of his body that he perceives as flawed. Continual unhappiness or dissatisfaction with a part of one's body will almost certainly have a negative effect on one's body image. Such persistent, negative feelings about a part of one's body can in rare cases escalate to a psychiatric disorder known as body dysmorphic disorder. A person suffering from body dysmorphic disorder focuses excessively on a part of the body that he perceives as flawed.

A person with a body dysmorphic disorder is obsessively dissatisfied with her body.

Can I Change the Way I Look?

A person with body dysmorphic disorder does not perceive himself accurately.

Often in body dysmorphic disorder the bodily flaw is actually imagined, and yet the person cannot be convinced of his body's true state.

Not every person who worries about part of her body has a psychiatric disorder. If so, we would all be diagnosed with these disorders! To be diagnosed as having body dysmorphic disorder, the focus on the body part must be so severe that it significantly impacts the person's life and impairs her ability to function normally. Furthermore, if a person's body obsession is related to or part of a different physical or psychiatric disorder, then the person would not be diagnosed as having body dysmorphic disorder.

A patient with body dysmorphic disorder does not see her body part as simply flawed, but begins to regard even the slightest irregularities as serious deformities. This **preoccupation** with her perceived deformities can dominate all other considerations in her life. She will begin to think that other people are as preoccupied with her "deformities" as she is. Perhaps she will think that other people are always looking at her, talking about her, or laughing at her ugliness. Her social interactions and relationships will suffer, and she may even become **delusional** about her body.

The most common body parts that people with body dysmorphic disorder focus on are characteristics of the head or face, specifically on the shape of the nose, mouth, teeth, eyes, and eyebrows or on scars, wrinkles, and hair loss. It is also common, however, for a woman to focus on her breasts, genitals, and hips and for a man to focus on the size or function of his penis. Not surprisingly, body dysmorphic disorder occurs more commonly in image-oriented North America than in parts of the world that do not have such a powerful media. Perhaps surprising, however, is the fact that, at least in North

America, men and women appear to suffer from body dysmorphic disorder in roughly equal numbers.

A person with body dysmorphic disorder will not feel better about himself after having a makeover. This is because he cannot see the true reality of his body. In essence, it makes no difference what his body looks like, because the only way he can see his body is as ugly or flawed. These flaws, however, are largely in his mind. Even if his body does have a true physical irregularity that could be perceived as a flaw, the seriousness of that irregularity is misconstrued by his mind. Simply "fixing" the body part, therefore, will not cure the person of his body woes. A person with body dysmorphic disorder does not need a makeover. He needs assistance from a professional, like a doctor, psychiatrist, or therapist, who can treat the issues that are more than skin deep.

Dying to Be Thin: Anorexia Nervosa

Hannah regarded herself in the mirror. For ten torturous minutes, she stood naked, fearfully watching Mirror Girl. Puffing her chipmunk cheeks, Mirror Girl stared back defiantly, her double chin dangling. Hannah cringed, sucked in her breath, and turned to examine her profile. Mirror Girl's stomach bulged as she smiled menacingly. Hannah turned back and glared at Mirror Girl's wide hips, then nearly cried as Mirror Girl wiggled her fat sausage thighs. Everything about Mirror Girl made Hannah feel sick. She was a blimp—swollen and completely out of control. Today, Hannah vowed, today she would

Anorexia affects both males and females.

do whatever it took to make herself thin and banish Mirror Girl forever.

Hannah stepped away from her image and onto the scale. The red needle swung, and Hannah choked back tears. One hundred and five pounds. Disgusting. She felt completely ashamed. Sure that somewhere Mirror Girl was laughing, Hannah dressed quickly, layering thick bulky clothes over her body to hide her fat from view.

When Hannah entered the kitchen, her mother looked her over with an appraising eye.

"Hannah, why do you bury yourself under all those frumpy clothes? You have such a pretty figure," she admonished. "I would have died to be so skinny when I was your age." She held two waffles out as she spoke.

Hannah barely heard what her mother said. She stared at the waffles while a familiar panic rose in her chest. Her breath quickening, Hannah hesitated for a moment, then snatched the waffles from her mother's hand.

"I gotta run," Hannah murmured, wrapping the waffles in a paper napkin. Before her mother could say more, Hannah sprinted out the door.

Hannah could feel her fear growing as she walked briskly down the sidewalk. She held the waffles gingerly away from her body as if they were something dangerous. Her eyes darted back and forth, searching. She grew more desperate as she imagined the fat in the waffles. She glanced around more furtively. She could practically feel the pounds seeping through her hands, penetrating her skin, and moving right to her monstrous thighs. Finally she saw what she was looking for. Hannah ran to the garbage can and breathing a sigh of relief threw the waffles in.

In the above example, Hannah, who is in most ways a typical North American teen, suffers from a severely distorted body image. When she looks in the mirror, she truly sees chipmunk cheeks, a double chin, and a fat stomach and thighs. But in reality, Hannah is very thin, perhaps even dangerously so. What she sees in the mirror is not the way her body actually looks. She only weighs 105 pounds, nearly forty pounds less than the average North American woman. Nevertheless, Hannah sees herself as fat, tries to hide her body, fears food, and refuses to eat.

Hannah's distorted body image is part of a serious medical condition, but it is not body dysmorphic disorder. Instead, Hannah suffers from a dangerous and common eating disorder called anorexia nervosa.

The most defining characteristics of anorexia nervosa are self-starvation and extreme, often-rapid weight loss. People suffering from anorexia nervosa tend to, like Hannah, have a distorted perception of their body's size and appearance. People with this condition will severely limit their food intake and often engage in excessive amounts of exercise to burn off any calories they do take in. If a person has anorexia nervosa, she may also display intense fear of gaining weight or even fear of food.

> Between five and twenty of every one hundred people suffering from anorexia nervosa will lose their lives to the disease.

The health risks of anorexia nervosa are extremely serious. If untreated, this condition can cause permanent damage to the body and even death. Some of the most common effects of anorexia nervosa are fatigue, bad breath, weakening of the bones, dehydration, kidney damage, muscle loss, heart damage, hair loss, ***cessation***

of periods in women, and growing a layer of fine, downy hair all over the body (an attempt by the emaciated body to stay warm). Many people think that anorexia nervosa only affects girls and women, but this is untrue. Girls and women do experience anorexia nervosa at a far greater rate, but boys and men are increasingly presenting with the disease. The condition most commonly develops in the early teenage years. Like body dysmorphic disorder, the poor body image that people with anorexia nervosa have cannot be cured with a makeover. Medical treatment is needed.

Bulimia Nervosa

Bulimia nervosa is another serious and relatively common eating disorder that is related to a distorted body image. People with bulimia also tend to believe they are overweight and feel intense fear of food, fat, and weight gain. However, whereas in anorexia nervosa the defining characteristics are self-starvation and weight loss, the defining characteristic of bulimia is a pattern of bingeing usually followed by purging.

When a person binges on food, he consumes a huge amount of food in a very short space of time. During a bingeing event, a person might consume five times the amount of food that a person would otherwise eat in an entire day. The person bingeing appears to lose control during these events, and finds himself unable to stop the compulsive eating. When the bingeing ends, however, the person feels extreme remorse and depression. Sickened by his own behavior or frightened of the weight he will gain from the excessive caloric intake, the person then endeavors to rid his body of everything he consumed. To accomplish this, the person may force himself to vomit, take *laxatives*, engage in extremely strenuous exercise, or abuse diet pills. A person with bulimia generally recognizes that his bingeing and purging pattern is abnormal and out of control, yet he feels powerless to stop it.

Approximately 7 million females and 1 million males in the United States have eating disorders.

People with bulimia nervosa do not tend to have the same weight loss or emaciation that commonly accompanies anorexia nervosa. A person can suffer with bulimia for years yet never appear sick or too thin to her family and friends. Nevertheless, like anorexia nervosa, bulimia is a dangerous condition that can permanently alter one's health and even cause death. Some of the side effects of bulimia include damaged teeth, bad breath, burned esophagus, irritated lungs, dehydration, muscle weakness, seizures, and kidney damage. The most common cause of death among people with bulimia is heart failure due to a *depletion* of minerals like potassium and sodium. In bulimia nervosa, death is often sudden and completely unexpected. Like anorexia nervosa, bulimia occurs far more commonly among women, but rates appear to be rising among men. Also like anorexia nervosa, the distorted body images, depression, and persistent negative feelings that people with bulimia suffer from cannot be fixed by physical alterations like makeovers. These issues need to be addressed by trained medical professionals.

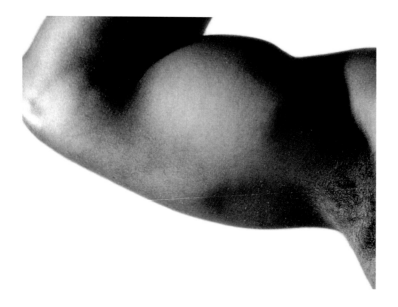

Men may be willing to take chemicals in order to increase the size of their muscles.

Steroid Use

While eating disorders like anorexia nervosa, bulimia, and other attempts to control weight and stay thin are common among women, large numbers of men suffer in the opposite extreme. These men, spurred by an obsession with making their bodies big, turn not just to behaviors like bodybuilding and nutritional supplements, but to using controlled substances known as anabolic steroids.

Anabolic steroids are synthetic chemicals that, when put in the body, act similarly to male sex hormones like testosterone. The major effect that anabolic steroids can produce is growth of the muscle tissues. The only way to legally obtain steroids is through a prescription, but a huge illegal drug trade has grown out of selling steroids to athletes and others who wish to grow bigger, stronger muscles.

Using anabolic steroids can have unpleasant side effects. The most common of these side effects is an increase in male characteristics like body hair and a deepening voice. These side effects may be difficult to detect in men, but they are usually quite noticeable in women who abuse steroids. Breast growth and shrinking testicles are common side effects in men. Male-patterned baldness, acne, aggressive behavior, and rage are also common side effects that occur in both men and women. Life-threatening side effects may include heart attack and liver cancer. Most effects of steroid use reverse after one ceases taking the substances, but some side effects, like baldness, can be irreversible. It is also unclear what the long-term side effects of prolonged steroid use might be. Typically, your body produces the proper amount of hormones it needs and regulates its production depending on how many hormones are active in the body. When you take steroids, you disrupt your body's natural production of hormones by flooding your body with excessive amounts of chemicals. Your endocrine system, the body system involved in the manufacture of hor-

> During the 1990s, steroid use among teenage boys leveled off and was even reduced in some places. However, steroid use among teenage girls appears to have doubled.

97

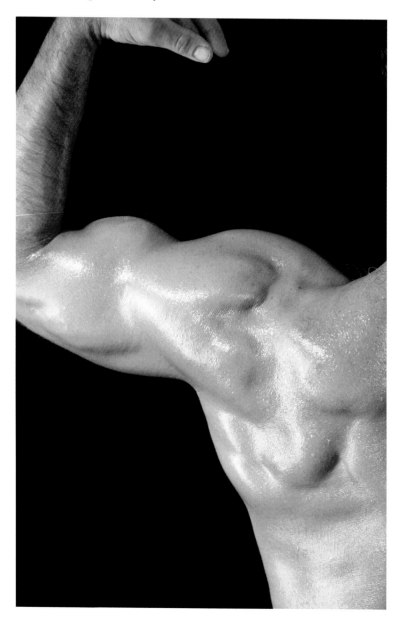

Big muscles are not worth risking your health!

mones, then ceases its own natural production. Studies have not yet determined what the long-term effects of such system shutdowns will be.

Steroid use was once limited to the medical field where steroids can treat some forms of illness. Illegal use and abuse of steroids then spread to professional athletes who realized they could enhance strength and performance with these drugs. However, over the past three decades steroid use has been steadily rising in the larger population, and it is no longer limited to the community of professional athletes. Steroid abuse now **permeates** all levels of the population. Using steroids as part of a training program became disturbingly common among high school and college athletes in the 1980s. Throughout the 1990s, the growth rate of steroid use in high schools leveled off. Currently, it is holding relatively constant. One reason given for the halt in growth rates is the availability of legal supplements like creatine. Another factor is education programs which have taught young people about the dangers of steroids. Nearly all competitive sports are now forced to test athletes for steroid use, and the underground trade of the drugs is now quite common in fitness facilities and recreation centers. Many female athletes take steroids, but it is almost exclusively men who engage in steroid use outside of sports. Many researchers blame North American society's focus on the super male image for this disturbing trend.

6

EXTREME MAKEOVER:
The Dreams and the Risks

Y ou've heard about them on the radio. You've seen them on TV. You've read about them in magazines: extreme makeovers—where "ugly" people, "fat" people, un-happy people, and unsuc-cessful people go under the knife to change their looks and hopefully their lives. They emerge from surgery bruised, bloodied, swollen, in pain, and held together by layers of white bandages. For a moment, the horror seems impossible, but then they emerge like butterflies from cocoons. They are unrecognizable, beautiful, new, and most importantly, they are happy.

So-called extreme makeovers are definitely prevalent in our society today. Such makeovers are the subject of everything from books to television shows. Like other beauty aids and makeover techniques we have discussed, extreme makeovers are a billion-dollar industry. What makes these makeovers "extreme" is the use of surgery to enhance beauty. Surgery can alter a person's looks in dramatic ways, and skilled surgeons can definitely enhance certain peoples' beauty, but are the glowing examples of happily made-over people on TV real?

Are extreme makeovers really all they are cracked up to be? Will beauty in the twenty-first century come from a knife rather than from a body or bottle?

Plastic surgery is a name given to surgery whose purpose is to sculpt, mold, shape, or reshape the body. Plastic surgery's focus is usually on the body's appearance rather than on the body's function. There are two types of plastic surgery: reconstructive and cosmetic. Plastic surgery is most commonly used to correct things like birth defects, improve a person's appearance after a disfiguring accident or illness, or enhance a person's physical attributes for greater beauty. Reconstructive surgery is an important field of medicine and has helped millions of people recover and live happier lives after terrible illnesses and accidents. Here, however, we will mostly consider cosmetic surgery—surgery performed specifically for the purpose of enhancing beauty rather than to correct a birth defect or disfigurement, because this is the type of surgery generally used in extreme forms of makeovers.

The most common reason given by doctors for *elective* cosmetic surgery is to enhance appearance for the purpose of improving body image and self-esteem. In years past, there was a great deal of *stigma* attached to having elective cosmetic surgery. People who did so were often seen as vain and *frivolous*. Today, however, as more people have benefited from cosmetic surgery, much of the stigma has faded. What was once done almost exclusively by wealthy people and kept secret is now openly discussed and sought by many.

It is still relatively rare for doctors to perform purely cosmetic surgery on people under age eighteen. Nevertheless, the number of cosmetic surgeries performed on this age group is growing every year. The numbers of men getting cosmetic procedures are also on the rise.

Can I Change the Way I Look?

When cosmetic surgery is performed on young people, the most common procedures are otoplasty (pinning back the ears), rhinoplasty (nose reshaping), breast reduction in both girls and boys, and breast augmentation in girls.

There are a number of very important things you should consider if you are a young person who is thinking about cosmetic surgery. The first is that if you are under eighteen, your body is still probably growing. Even if you have already reached your full height, other parts of your body, like your facial bones, your muscles, and your sex organs, are still developing and changing. You may not like the way you look now, but that doesn't mean you won't like the way your body will look in the future. When you are growing, some parts of your body will reach full maturity before other parts. This can make you feel awkward and out of proportion, but it doesn't mean you'll be like this forever. For example, an extremely common complaint heard from teenagers is, "My nose is too big." It makes sense, however, that young people would think their noses look big because a person's nose typically reaches full development before the rest of the face finishes growing and fills out. Despite their initial unhappiness, most people find that they eventually "grow into" their nose and are satisfied with the way it looks. Running out and getting a nose job at sixteen would typically be a bad idea. Nevertheless, rhinoplasty is one of the most common procedures performed on teens. A similar situation exists in the case of breast implants. Many young women wish that their breasts were larger, but as a teenager, your breasts probably have not finished developing. Breast implants and the health risks and complications that can come with them don't make sense for a young person who may not even be done growing.

The American Society of Plastic Surgeons reports that in 2002 in the United States, 223,673 people under the age of eighteen underwent cosmetic plastic surgery. A further 51,734 young people underwent nonsurgical cosmetic procedures.

Plastic surgery can significantly alter a person's appearance, and if the person likes the changes, the effects of plastic surgery can contribute to more positive self-esteem. However, there is currently a disturbing trend among some medical professionals and people in the media who claim that plastic surgery is a good tool for helping young people develop positive self-esteem. According to them, plastic surgery is the new cure-all for everything that ails a young person's confidence and emotions. Their argument is simple, if a young person hates the way he looks and thus feels unhappy and has low self-esteem, then changing the way he looks will make him happy, give him confidence, and help him develop high self-esteem. At first, this seems to make sense, but we should look a little closer. Weren't you always told that your self-esteem should be based on more than your looks? Didn't anyone ever tell you that your inner qualities, like being smart, funny, kind, determined, or energetic, were much more valuable than your looks? Shouldn't self-esteem be built upon these deep and long-lasting personality traits and abilities rather than on something as relative and temporary as beauty?

People who claim that plastic surgery and makeovers are proper avenues to building a positive body image and good self-esteem reinforce our society's emphasis on beauty and promote many of the same ideas that are so emotionally damaging to young people. It is one thing for an adult to have cosmetic surgery on a part of the body that causes emotional distress. But young people are still in the process of growing. Their bodies are changing every day, and their body image, self-esteem, and self-concept are in constant flux as well. Struggling through these changes and learning to accept one's new body are important parts of becoming an adult. A person's emotional and personal growth happens in stages, and most people pass through a stage of unhappiness and self-doubt before they reach the stage of self-acceptance and positive body image. Performing cosmetic surgery on a young person who is in the process of this normal life stage can rob that person of the future self-acceptance and self-image (self-acceptance and self-image that would have been based on more than just looks) he may have otherwise achieved. Cosmetic surgery might help a

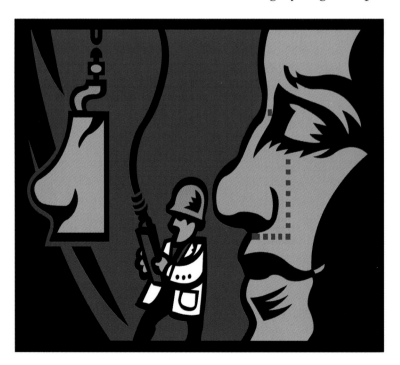

young person feel better about himself initially, but it could actually have a negative effect on self-esteem in the long term by reinforcing the notion that self-worth and happiness are connected to and dependent upon beauty. Sometimes people who have plastic surgery, but fail to deal with the deeper issues affecting their body image, self-esteem, and happiness, are disappointed when the surgery does not change their lives and focus on a different body part as the source of the problem. This can lead to a never-ending cycle of surgery in which the person is always convinced that just one more cosmetic procedure will make them happy, but afterwards always find a new body flaw to be dissatisfied with.

According to the American Society of Plastic Surgeons, during the 1990s in the United States, the rates of elective cosmetic procedures rose by more than 150 percent. Certain procedures, like breast augmentation, buttock lift, and upper-arm lift increased by more than 300 percent over the course of the decade.

Many people who think they want extreme makeovers don't understand that plastic surgery will only change them. It won't change other people. If your main goal is to have other people think about and treat you differently, plastic surgery cannot guarantee any success or improvement. Cosmetic surgery cannot make you look like someone else or insure success in areas of your life like relationships, school, or jobs. The physical changes that can result from plastic surgery can potentially improve self-esteem, but they can also complicate self-esteem issues. Cosmetic surgery is not appropriate for people, especially teens, who have very low self-esteem, because multiple issues cause low self-esteem, not just discomfort with a particular physical feature. Often people blame physical features for larger issues and unhappiness, but the truth is their unhappiness stems from more than just their looks. If you are considering cosmetic surgery, you need to ask yourself questions like, "Why do I want this surgery?" and "What do I expect this surgery to do for me?"

If you are absolutely certain that an "extreme makeover" is right for you, there are a number of steps you should take before having plastic surgery. The first is to understand the health risks, the most serious of which is the risk of death. Many plastic surgeries seem like simple procedures, and in some cases they are, but all surgeries carry with them a risk of death, even if that risk is remote. In the rare situations where death occurs, it is usually due to an unexpected complication of the surgery, such as complications with the **anesthesia** or the development of blood clots after surgery. All surgeries also carry the risk of infection. Forms of plastic surgery in which something is inserted into the body, like breast augmentation, chin implants, cheek implants, and some nose reconstructions, may carry a higher risk of infection than surgeries that don't implant something into the body. If you get a serious infection, or if your body rejects such an implant, you may need to have the implant removed. Infection increases the chances that you will need additional, costly surgeries. Other risks of plastic surgery include scarring, nerve damage in the altered area, poor results, and disappointment with the outcome of the alteration.

Most surgeons do their best to predict the outcome of surgery and communicate the possible outcomes to patients, but everyone's body is different. Each person reacts to surgery differently and heals differently. A doctor can't absolutely know the amount of scarring you will

Plastic surgeons cannot wave a magic wand and create the kind of person you long to be.

have or all the complications that could arise. Furthermore, though things like computer imaging are often used to show a patient what she can expect to look like after surgery, no doctor or computer program can know for sure what your outcome will be. You should keep in mind that all images you are shown of what you may look like after surgery are purely ***speculative***.

Unfortunately, another risk factor is that there are many untrustworthy doctors in the field of cosmetic surgery. Doctors can earn a lot of money from performing cosmetic procedures, and some doctors are more concerned with their pocketbooks, rather than their patients'

According to the American Society of Plastic Surgeons, nearly 6.6 million people had cosmetic surgery and 4.9 million people had nonsurgical cosmetic procedures in the United States in 2002.

interests. Currently, there are no laws or regulations in the United States requiring that a doctor have specialized training in plastic surgery to call herself a plastic surgeon. Always make sure that you know the background of your plastic surgeon. You should look for a doctor who is certified by the American Board of Plastic Surgery. This certification ensures that the doctor has completed five years of training for plastic surgery, two years of practice, and passed written and oral examinations. If you want to know if a plastic surgeon is certified by this board, you can call the Plastic Surgery Information Service at 1-800-

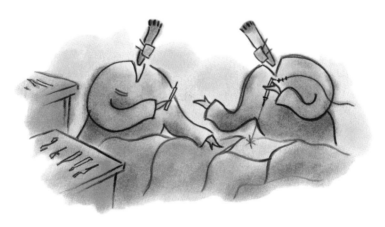

Before you undergo any surgery, be certain your doctor is well qualified.

635-0635. In Canada, you should make sure the plastic surgeon is certified by the Royal College of Physicians and Surgeons of Canada.

Many plastic surgeons today operate out of small, private offices where even surgeries are performed on-site rather than in a hospital. If you are considering a plastic surgeon who operates from this type of office, you should make sure that the office is very close to a hospital and that the doctor has a good relationship with it. No matter how simple a surgery, unexpected things can always go wrong. If something were to go wrong during your surgery, you would want to be sure that the staff and resources of a hospital are nearby to help.

7

A Makeover from the Inside Out

We've talked a lot about the emphasis on and importance of beauty in North American culture. We questioned what the word "makeover" means and some of the reasons people feel compelled to have makeovers. Additionally, we've looked at some of the many ways, from common cosmetics to drastic plastic surgery, that people try to improve their looks and considered the health risks associated with each of these makeover techniques. But now, let's look at one final question. Do makeovers have to be about changing the way a person looks, or can they be about changing something else?

What do you think would happen if, instead of people trying to change the way they look, people tried to change the way they think? What would our society be like if people cared more about the way they were inside than the way they appeared on the outside? What do you think people would consider beautiful if they questioned their **assumptions** about beauty and searched for it in places other than people's faces and bodies?

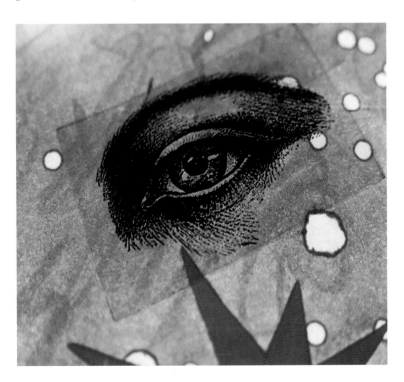

There is currently a growing movement of people in North America who are encouraging young people, not to get makeovers, but to ask the above questions and think about beauty in a different way. One example of this recent movement can be seen in a publishing company called New Moon® Publishing and an organization called Mind on the Media.

Each year at the same time that *People* magazine publishes its annual "50 Most Beautiful People," New Moon Publishing's small magazine, *New Moon: The Magazine for Girls and Their Dreams*, counteracts with its own list of beautiful people. Basing their decisions solely on essays written about the nominees rather than on photographs, *New Moon* selects twenty-five beautiful girls to be featured in the magazine for the wonderful qualities they have inside and great accomplishments they have achieved rather than the way that they look. Young women in the beautiful-girls issue haven't been models and actresses. They've done things like performed well in school, helped in their communities, and donated their hair to cancer victims. *New Moon* hopes that with each beautiful-girl issue, more young women will think about the way we measure beauty in our society and decide that their valuable personalities and abilities make them more beautiful than any extreme makeover ever could.

New Moon's focus on inner beauty has grown into an all-out public education campaign called "Turn Beauty Inside Out." This campaign seeks to educate people about the dangers of current representations of beauty in the media and searches for ways to encourage the notion of beauty as a quality that comes from inside rather than from physical appearance. This public education campaign is now overseen by an organization called Mind on the Media, which seeks to raise awareness about the images of women and girls portrayed in North American

media. You can learn more about Mind on the Media and the work that it does at www.mindonthemedia.org.

At the same time that awareness is growing about the pressures to be beautiful that young girls face and the emotional and psychological dangers of these pressures, some people are also realizing the similar pressures on boys. Recently, some doctors and educators have begun to speak out about the super male representations of masculinity on television and in other forms of the media. Hopefully there will soon be people and organizations lobbying for the interests of boys and young men as well.

The media is a powerful thing, and in North America it has been used to promote and sell physical representations of beauty. Perhaps someday soon, however, the media will also be used to teach young people that a makeover of one's physical body is not the only type of makeover a person can have. A person can also makeover her attitudes and beliefs. A person can question his assumptions about beauty and change the way he regards his body and the bodies of others. People can learn to value themselves for the people they are inside rather than the way that they look. Maybe we can all learn how to make ourselves over from the inside out.

Brumberg, Joan Jacobs. *The Body Project: An Intimate History of American Girls.* New York: Random House, 1997.

Erickson, Kim. *Drop-Dead Gorgeous: Protecting Yourself from the Hidden Dangers of Cosmetics.* New York: Contemporary Books, 2002.

Kirgerger, Kimberly. *No Body's Perfect: Stories by Teens about Body Image, Self-Acceptance, and the Search for Identity.* New York: Scholastic, 2003.

Luciano, Lynne. *Looking Good: Male Body Image in Modern America.* New York: Hill and Wang, 2001.

Moe, Barbara. *Understanding the Causes of a Negative Body Image.* New York: Rosen, 1999.

Nash, Joyce D. *What Your Doctor Can't Tell You About Cosmetic Surgery.* Oakland, Calif.: New Harbinger Publications, 1995.

Pipher, Mary. *Hunger Pains: The Modern Woman's Tragic Quest for Thinness.* New York: Ballantine, 1995.

Pipher, Mary. *Reviving Ophelia: Saving the Selves of Adolescent Girls.* New York: G.P. Putnam's Sons, 1994.

Pope, Harrison G., Katharine A. Phillips, and Roberto Olivardia. *The Adonis Complex: The Secret Crisis of Male Body Obsession.* New York: The Free Press, 2000.

Weatherford, M. Lisa. *Reconstructive and Cosmetic Surgery Sourcebook.* Detroit, Mich: Omnigraphics, 2001.

American Academy of Cosmetic Surgery
www.cosmeticsurgery.org

American Academy of Facial Plastic and Reconstructive Surgery, Inc.
www.aafprs.org

The Canadian Academy of Facial Cosmetic and Reconstructive Surgery
www.facialcosmeticsurgery.org

Canadian Society for Aesthetic Plastic Surgery
www.csaps.ca

Mind on the Media
www.mindonthemedia.org

The National Eating Disorders Association
www.nationaleatingdisorders.org

Plastic Surgery Information Service: 1-800-635-0635
www.plasticsurgery.org

The Renfrew Center Foundation
www.renfrew.org

Smart Plastic Surgery.com
www.smartplasticsurgery.com

Publisher's note:
The Web sites listed on this page were active at the time of publication. The publisher is not responsible for Web sites that have
changed their addresses or discontinued operation since the date of
publication. The publisher will review and update the Web sites
upon each reprint.

accessible Capable of being reached.

accumulates Gathers or piles up, especially little by little.

aerobics A system or program of physical exercise or conditioning designed to enhance circulation and respiratory efficiency that involves vigorous and sustained movement.

AIDS Acquired Immune Deficiency Syndrome; a serious, often fatal outcome of HIV.

aorta The great arterial trunk that carries blood from the heart to be distributed by branch arteries through the body.

anesthesia Loss of sensation with or without loss of consciousness.

assumptions Facts or statements taken for granted.

blood pressure The pressure exerted by the blood against the walls of the blood vessels, especially the arteries.

by-products Things produced in a usually industrial or biological process in addition to the principal products.

carbohydrate Any of various neutral compounds of carbon, hydrogen, and oxygen (as sugars, starches, and celluloses), most of which are formed by green plants and which constitute a major class of foods.

carcinogenic (CAR-sin-oh-jen-ik) Having a substance or agent producing or inciting cancer.

cash cow A steady and dependable source of income.

cessation A temporary or final stopping.

cumulative Increasing with each successive addition.

delusional Having a mental state marked by the occurrence of psychotic beliefs that mislead the mind or impair judgment.

depilatory (duh-PILL-uh-tor-ee) An agent for removing hair.

depletion The marked lessening of a substance in quantity, content, power, or value.

distorted Twisted out of the true meaning or proportion.

DNA Deoxyribonucleic acid which makes up the living genes, in the shape of strands coiled in a double helix shape, carrying and replicating the genetic information passed from generation to generation.

economic Having to do with money.

efficacy The power to produce a desired effect.

elective Involving a choice, optional; elective surgery is beneficial to the patient but not essential for survival.

electrolysis (ee-lek-TROL-i-sis) The destruction of hair roots with an electric current.

endorse To approve openly, especially to express support or approval of publicly and definitely.

Environmental Protection Agency A law enforcement agency in the United States that is charged with protection of the environment and regulation of some chemicals.

frivolous Of little importance, trivial, silly.

forum Place for discussion or expression of ideas.

genes The packages of hereditary information on a chromosome.

gurus (GOO-roos) People with exceptional knowledge or expertise in a particular subject.

HIV Human Immunodeficiency Virus; the virus that causes aids, transmitted through blood products and especially through sexual conduct.

hormones Products of living cells that circulate in body fluids and produce a specific effect on the activity of cells remote from their point of origin.

hydrogenated (hi-DROJ-en-ated) Combined or treated with or exposed to hydrogen.

idealized A high standard of perfection, beauty, or excellence.

immune system The bodily system that protects the body from foreign substances, cells, and tissues by producing the immune response.

infections Invasions by and multiplications of pathogenic microorganisms in body tissues.

inflammation A defensive reaction of the body's tissues to invasion by microorganisms or to the presence of a foreign body or other injury, accompanied by local swelling and pain and initial increased blood flow to the damaged part.

interventions Modifications, augmentations, to impose or intrude.

laxatives Usually mild drugs that loosen or relax, specifically to relieve constipation.

laser Any of several devices that convert incident electromagnetic radiation of mixed frequencies to one or more discrete frequencies of highly amplified and coherent ultraviolet, visible, or infrared radiation.

leach To empty, or to dissolve into something.

malnutrition Faulty and especially inadequate intake and utilization of food substances.

masculine Male; having qualities appropriate to or usually associated with a man.

maturation (MA-chur-a-shun) The emergence of personal and behavioral characteristics through growth processes.

metabolism The sum of the processes in the buildup and destruction of protoplasm.

multifaceted Having many definable aspects that

make up a subject (as of contemplation) or an object (as of consideration).

musculatures The muscles of all or parts of an animal body.

neurological Relating to the nervous system, especially in respect to its structure, functions, and abnormalities.

obsession Compulsive and usually unreasonable preoccupation with something that is often accompanied by anxiety.

osteoporosis (AH-stee-oh-pore-oh-sis) A condition that especially affects older women and is characterized by decrease in bone mass with decreased density and enlargement of bone spaces producing porosity and fragility.

overzealous Filled with or characterized by extreme eagerness and ardent interest in pursuit of something.

perceives To become aware of or believe something based on your own thoughts and observations.

permeates Pervades, flows throughout, spreads through.

political Of or relating to government, or the conduct of government.

preoccupation Something that engrosses and absorbs all of the attention of the mind.

retardant Serving or tending to slow up, especially by preventing or hindering advance or accomplishment.

saturated Pure, as fat.

scarification (SCAR-if-i-ca-shun) The act or process of making scratches or small cuts in (as the skin) that result in permanent marks.

secular Of or relating to the worldly or earthly life; not overtly or specifically religious.

sedentary Doing or requiring much sitting, doing little exercise.

speculative Involving, based on, or constituting intellectual speculation; theoretical rather than demonstrable.

stigma A mark of shame or discredit.

synonymous (sin-ON-i-mus) Alike in meaning or significance.

synthetic Produced artificially; not naturally occurring.

toxic Poisonous.

trans fat A type of hydrogenated dietary fat contained in margarines and commercial cooking oils that are bad for health because they are known to raise cholesterol levels.

tumultuous Marked by turbulence or upheaval.

Type II diabetes Adult-onset diabetes, sometimes precipitated by obesity.

unattainable Incapable of reaching, unachievable.

upper classes Social classes occupying a position above the mid-class.

U.S. Food and Drug Administration A law enforcement agency in the United States which inspects, tests, and sets standards for foodstuffs, medicines, and medical devices, and is also involved with the regulations governing associated products and locations that might affect personal health.

UV Ultraviolet light; of or relating to a range of invisible radiation wavelengths that are just beyond the violet in the visible spectrum.

125

126

PICTURE CREDITS

Autumn Libal received her degree from Smith College in Northampton, Massachusetts. A former water-aerobics instructor, she now dedicates herself exclusively to writing for young people. Other Mason Crest series she has contributed to include PSYCHIATRIC DISORDERS: DRUGS & PSYCHOLOGY FOR THE MIND AND BODY and YOUTH WITH SPECIAL NEEDS. She has also written health-related articles for *New Moon: The Magazine for Girls and Their Dreams.*

Mary Ann McDonnell, APRN, BC, is an advanced practice nurse, the director of the clinical trials program in pediatric psychopharmacology research at Massachusetts General Hospital, has a private practice in pediatric psychopharmacology, and is a clinical instructor for Northeastern University and Boston College advanced practice nursing students. Her areas of expertise are bipolar disorder in children and adolescents, ADHD, and depression. Mary Ann is one of a small group of advanced practice nurses working in pediatric psychopharmacology research and practice, who has a national reputation as an expert advanced practice nurse in the field of pediatric bipolar disorder, ADHD, and depression. She sits on the institutional review board and the research education committee at Massachusetts General Hospital and is a lecturer for local and national educational conferences on bipolar disorder, depression, and ADHD.

Dr. Sara Forman graduated from Barnard College and Harvard Medical School. She completed her residency in Pediatrics at Children's Hospital of Philadelphia and a fellowship in Adolescent Medicine at Children's Hospital Boston (CHB). She currently is an attending in Adolescent Medicine at CHB, where she has served as Director of the Adolescent Outpatient Eating Disorders Program for the past nine years. She has also consulted for the National Eating Disorder Screening Project on its high school initiative and has presented at many conferences about teens and eating disorders. In addition to her clinical and administrative roles in the Eating Disorders Program, Dr. Forman teaches medical students and residents and coordinates the Adolescent Medicine rotation at CHB. Dr. Forman sees primary care adolescent patients in the Adolescent Clinic at CHB, at Bentley College, and at the Germaine Lawrence School, a residential school for emotionally disturbed teenage girls.